Heaven, Science,
and the Last Things

Heaven, Science,
and the Last Things

COLIN CRASTON

RESOURCE *Publications* · Eugene, Oregon

HEAVEN, SCIENCE, AND THE LAST THINGS

Resource Publications
An Imprint of Wipf and Stock Publishers
199 W. 8th Ave., Suite 3
Eugene, OR 97401

www.wipfandstock.com

ISBN 978-1-61097-031-0

Manufactured in the U.S.A.

In memory of those I have known now in heaven

Contents

Foreword

STEVEN WEINBERG, renowned physicist and Nobel Prize winner once remarked: "The more the universe seems comprehensible, the more it seems pointless." This disturbing comment might well seem to be the "credo" of many intelligent people today. They, and we, look at the world with all its beauty and order—because nothing would work without the laws of the universe that hold all together—and yet wonder at the evil and disorder that question the idea that human beings have a special place within creation. Colin Craston addresses these questions in this short but comprehensible and impressive book.

But Colin himself is an impressive man. Now in his ninth decade, he has not stopped thinking, reading, reflecting, and being. When I was Archbishop of Canterbury, Colin was Chairman of the Anglican Consultative Council, a body that presided over the workings of the Anglican Communion. In that position he demonstrated his ability to think clearly and to suggest routes through difficult questions with ease, humour and intelligence.

It is not surprising, therefore, that he approaches the most difficult issue of the "meaning" of the Christian faith in a world confused about what it believes, with his customary insight and wide reading. What is important to realise is that Dr. Craston is not trying to "prove" the existence of God, because we all know now that is impossible, as is the case with the non-existence of God. The argument of this book is that the Christian faith offers a credible and cogent meaning to the deepest questions that trouble us, because the God and Father of Jesus Christ is also the Finisher of all things. Believing in God the Finisher gives fresh hope and meaning to our lives and this, in turn, reinforces the conviction that God will have the last word. Julian of Norwich summed it up: "All shall be well, and all shall be well, and all manner of things shall be well."

GEORGE CAREY

The Most Reverend and Right Hon. The Lord Carey of Clifton
Lord Carey is the 103rd Archbishop of Canterbury 1991–2002

Preface

MINISTERING IN different congregations in my retirement I have come across Christian believers who are puzzled by the relationship of science and faith. They feel committed to belief in the return of Christ and in a Day of Judgment, and affirm these beliefs when they say the creeds. Yet, they hear from the media and remember from science lessons at school amazing (and possibly contradictory) predictions about the future of our planet and indeed of the whole universe. How can Christian belief in the Last Things fit in with the idea that the universe is likely to go on for billions of years? Must believers choose between science and faith?

Many may not get around to reading the works of renowned scientists like Professor John Polkinghorne, a physicist and Anglican priest—to whom, this author owes much—or to studying the theological works of a great Christian thinker like Bishop N. T. Wright, who has inspired me profoundly, particularly in my retirement. This book is an attempt to pass on to other believers the thoughts and reflections that have strengthened my hope in God's future purposes.

Introduction

IN MY late eighties, I am in heaven's waiting room. I want to stay with my loved ones and friends, and be of some usefulness as long as I am allowed. But when my time comes, entering more fully into heaven will be a great adventure.

"Heaven," and its opposite "hell," are words frequently heard. Mostly they are used to describe personal experiences in life. Passing through some tragedy or terror is described as hell. Achieving some enjoyable hope is heaven. Thus the concepts are essentially centered on self. And, given the current tendency to exaggerate in communication, both in the media and in personal reactions, the two words are frequently seized upon. Former generations could be conditioned to exercise restraint, to refrain from making a fuss. Now it is a case of letting it all out.

There is, however, a more traditional use of the concept of heaven, relating to departed loved ones. Unless atheistic or agnostic views are held, bereaved relatives cling to the hope that the departed has gone to heaven. In spite of the secularization of society many still entertain a vague idea of God and some existence after death.

Sentiment plays a significant part. The loved one is now at peace. Father has joined Mother. When the pleasures of this life are somehow still to be enjoyed, the idea of extinction at death is too hard to contemplate. Compared with this life, heaven is still thought of by many as second-best. In a recent interview on TV, a lady distressed by the murder of a younger woman said, "she has gone to heaven; she didn't deserve this!"

The idea of an after-life developed early on in human history. In the evolution of *Homo sapiens* from other primate species, growing self-consciousness began to contemplate a world beyond this one. Supernatural beings were thought of as being responsible for natural phenomena such as the seasons, and indeed for harmful events. These spirits, unseen but located in nature, had to be placated at some cost. Once the spirit world had captured human imagination the wish for an afterlife developed. This can be observed in the care that was taken with burial practices. Where possible, treasures or useful instruments were included with the corpses, indicating the belief that these treasures would be needed in an afterlife. Outstanding examples of these practices survive from ancient Egypt.

World religions as they emerged had their distinctive concepts of the supernatural and the human relationship to it. The three monotheistic religions, Judaism, Christianity, and Islam, have some features in common but also distinctive differences. Adherents base their beliefs on their interpretation of the respective sacred Scriptures. In the following chapters, I will explore what Christian Scripture says about heaven, and so here we turn to the matter of scriptural interpretation.

1

Using Scriptures

IN ADDRESSING Scripture there is always the tendency to find what we want to find. Readers are pre-conditioned by their own desires, convictions, and prejudices to seek self-confirmation. This can have some damaging consequences. Fanatical Muslim extremists can be motivated towards suicide bombing by the conviction that their faith promises immediate entrance to paradise where they will be welcomed by young virgin women. More widely, adherents to Islam will support death by stoning for adulterers or hand-severance as punishment for theft. Believers in Christian Scripture are also liable to harmful interpretations of the texts. When two hundred years ago some Christians strived to end the slave trade and later, the institution of slavery, other Christians argued that the New Testament condoned slavery. As the church reaped financial benefit from slavery, many were predisposed to find justification for it in Scripture. Throughout church history there have been instances of interpretations of Scripture now rejected as harmful.

A powerful influence on the way Scripture is used is the culture of its readers. Indeed, the effect of culture on religion generally is profound but not easily recognized. Culture shapes our lives, our attitudes and aspirations. In the Western world, growing affluence and consumerism can blind minds to the truth that Christ challenges culture, approving what accords with his kingdom but condemning what is opposed. Thus, fundamentalist Christian groups in the USA can present a strong message that discipleship with Christ will assure economic prosperity. Verses in the Psalms are alleged to support this. Certainly considerable affluence for their leaders is assured. In Latin American culture, the plight of vast numbers in poverty and oppression has led to the gospel being seen as primarily liberation for the poor. That indeed is part of the gospel, but not the whole. The church across the world is made up of very many diverse cultures. It is inevitable that interpretation of the Scriptures will be influenced by prevailing cultural conditions. The challenge is to seek a balance in conjunction with Christians elsewhere.

Everyone who comes to the Christian Scriptures comes with assumptions; generally shaped by the particular tradition they find themselves in. In the very conservative evangelical tradition a reader may regard every sentence, every word as directly inspired by God. Although the word "dictation" may not be used the inference is that the Holy Spirit controlled the human writers throughout the writing process. A problem not faced in this view is that we have a range of manuscripts with some variations; the original documents being lost forever. It cannot be satisfactory to argue that the original documents were preserved from all error. If God preserved the original documents from error, then why not the copying of manuscripts over the centuries following? And, if the original recipient of God's revelation was so controlled by the Holy Spirit, what of those who edited the books later? Some editing is apparent in parts of Scripture.

Biblical scholars are not free from approaching their studies with assumptions. One cannot rule out the possibility that like experts in other fields, they may be motivated by a desire for notoriety by the theories they expound and publicize in books, for which they desire good sales. Something new and dramatic gains recognition. But even if motivation is as pure as can be—and after sixty years in the ministry, I can recognize the problem of motivation—there are other assumptions with which scholars may approach their task. Some will treat the Scriptures just as any other ancient book: to be dissected, its contents related to other sources, a product entirely human in origin. Others, while not going so far, will regard the element of miracle in the text as at least suspect. The assumption is almost that miracles do not happen. So, where they are reported in the text, writer or editors have introduced them to make a theological point. In particular, stories of Jesus' miracles have been introduced to convince people in the early days of the church of the truth of Christianity. The tendency in this approach is to be selective. Miracles of healing are more acceptable, though some more natural explanation may be possible. Nature miracles, like stilling of a storm on the lake, are seen as more suspect.

Undoubtedly there are differences in accounts of events between the four Gospels. Some are not easy to reconcile. But truly, witnesses of events are struck by different features. No one person's account of what happened is ever exactly the same as another person's. There is another factor to bear in mind. Much of Scripture began as oral tradition, that is, what God had revealed in particular situations was passed down by word of mouth before appearing in written form. In what was eventually written down, the writer would emphasize what was seen to be particularly relevant to readers in their contemporary situations. For example, Mark would draw out implications for a Gentile readership in specific circumstances the evangelist had in mind. Similarly, Matthew would have had a Jewish readership in mind. This would not have been regarded as being unfaithful to the tradition, because the tradition was not regarded as fixed exclusively in the past. There is abundant evidence that New Testament writers treated the Old Testament Scriptures in the same way. While Jesus accepted the Bible he knew as conveying the authority of God, he adapted certain aspects of the Old Testament—important directions, such as Sabbath observance, food regulations (clean or unclean) and divorce provisions. Similarly, Paul dealt radically with circumcision, observance of special days, and diet regulations. It all adds up to the truth that passing on the revelation of God was a living tradition.

Why all the foregoing about different uses of Scripture in a book about heaven? Because what follows is an attempt to find what can be said of heaven in Scripture. Therefore, the approach adopted needs to be set out, so that the reader can assess it. As we have seen, no interpretation of Scripture by any individual or church tradition is infallible.

The approach to Scripture in this book is as follows. God, over centuries, has revealed his truth in order to accomplish his purposes. Supremely, he has revealed himself in the Incarnation, Death, and Resurrection of Jesus Christ. All that God revealed before Christ was in preparation for that decisive intervention. In the New Testament we have the record of Christ's earthly life, and after the Resurrection the exposition of God's saving act given to the apostles.

The revelation before Christ was inevitably of a progressive nature. Thus, what was partial, incomplete, needs to be seen as such and supplemented by what is later. What was perceived as God's will in, say, the time of the wilderness wanderings is not necessarily his will for this people now. Many of the over six hundred commands in the Law of Moses have now been left behind.

Whatever revelation God imparted to human recipients in any age was inevitably within the culture and understanding of the time. It could not be otherwise if it was to be intelligible. There may be more than the recipient understood, but its immediate relevance had to be grasped. So, we must recognize both divine initiative and human understanding, and in the latter, fallibility. In this a clear distinction must be drawn between the Incarnation and Scripture. The Incarnation is the Word of God in a human being, a perfect blend of divinity and humanity. As we believe Jesus was without sin, so he was without error in his deeds and words. That is not to say that in his Incarnation he knew everything. As God the Son, he had laid aside his glory, accepting humility as human, as indeed a serving slave. But what he offered was without sin or error as the Word incarnate. But the word written in Scripture is not of the same nature as the Incarnation. Its recipients were not infallible. We need to recognize where what they wrote reflects the culture and limited understanding of their time. An illustration of this approach to the Scriptures, which has relevance to the theme of this book, is in the way the apostles understood human physical death. Regarding the early chapters of Genesis as a record of literal history they were bound to see human death as a consequence of the Fall. They would also see death in a spiritual sense as separation from God. In that we still believe with them. The effect of sin is to separate us from God who is perfectly holy. But in modern times we have to face the truth that the pattern for everything in the universe since the beginning has been birth, life, decay, death. We die because everything in creation dies—stars, planets, plant life, animal species, human beings. We have the same kind of genes, organs, and life systems as other sub-human species. To be a creature is to be mortal.

Without doubt, the Death and Resurrection of Jesus affords the answer, indeed the conquest of death—in the spiritual sense of separation from God, of physical death in the hope of resurrection, and in what may be called its moral sense of "dying to sin and rising to new life" in Christ, sacramentally figured in baptism. So in interpreting a passage like Paul's fifteenth chapter of 1 Corinthians we bear in mind these different senses.

The foregoing illustrates the truth that interpretation of Scripture in modern times can differ from that of former ages. God has allowed truth about the universe and human nature to be discovered which writers in Scripture and readers in centuries afterwards could not know. All truth is God's truth, pointing to the reality of who he is, what he has done, and still is doing. Biblical truth needs to be seen as congruous with all other truth. Human reason, submitting prayerfully to the Holy Spirit's guidance, must pursue the search.

In all scriptural writings, the genre has to be distinguished. There is straightforward historical account; poetry; myth or parable, meaning stories conveying religious truth; stories relating to events in history or nature or life situations. There is also the genre known as apocalyptic. It is language aimed at describing the future, the Last Things and heaven. The unseen world now or in the next life, can only be spoken of in terms of what is known in this world of time and space. The book of the Revelation of John the Divine abounds with descriptions of events and objects in terms of this world. Streets of gold, gates of pearl, creatures with strange features are presented. It can only be a mistake to take these pictorial images literally, a mistake often made by fundamentalist Christians, Jehovah's Witnesses and others. There is a strange fascination in wanting to predict the future by a literal use of this kind of text. Paul reminds us that here we "see through a glass darkly." We do not know everything we would wish to know through Scripture. However, we know enough to realize God's salvation of us and how we may enter that salvation.

2

Eternity and God

THE CONCEPT of eternity is beyond our grasp. The tendency is to think of it as unending time. The word "everlasting" is taken as a synonym for eternity, but it also conveys the sense of time. Time and space are of the essence of our created universe, subject to natural laws that create variations. If the universe ends, as it had a beginning, time will cease. Eternity is not what goes on happening after that.

The Bible is not a book of science. But its overall theme suggests eternity is a present reality. It is—we can only use human language—the reality of God. It is beyond time, but it intervenes in time. Even the word "realm" is inadequate, as it suggests spatial dimension. Another category drawn from human experience is that of kingdom. Eternity is God's kingdom. In modern times the concept of kingdom is less favored, as democratic rule is preferred to the power of one individual. But if God exists he must be supreme over all that is. (The use of the male personal pronoun is not to be taken as implying gender. The use of "he/she" would be tedious; the use of "it" would not reflect the Bible's theme.) So, the concept of eternity depends on the existence of God.

Whether God does or does not exist can never be proved, if the kind of proof in mind is scientific, such as can be applied to mathematics. Whether to believe or not is a choice individuals must make. Atheists, who are becoming more strident and offensive to all religion, believe that because God's existence cannot be proved by scientific methods, he cannot exist. They need to recognize that it is impossible to prove a negative. The most it is possible to claim is that they see no evidence in science in favor of God's existence. Science, however, does not—cannot—offer a complete knowledge of everything that is, or why anything exists. There are descriptions that are accurate, theories that are practically certain to reflect reality, unanswered questions and problems. Thus, scientific exploration goes on.

Starved of conclusive proof of the non-existence of God, atheists resort to drawing attention to evil things done in the name of religion or the more bizarre beliefs and practices of different faiths. Richard Dawkins, the Oxford professor, is fond of this line of attack in his books and journalism. There is no point in denying that down the centuries people of different religions have pursued cruel and dangerous practices. And in every faith can be found views held by some that defy reason and distort the faith they profess. This point has already been made in the section on using Scripture.

So, why should it be reasonable to believe in God and to accept that faith as a basis for life? Inevitably the following is a personal story drawn from a lifetime's experience. Over the course of history so-called proofs for the existence of God have been offered. Individually and collectively they do not amount to proof of the kind scientists require in their fields. However, they do afford the possibility of God's existence, which is reasonable to accept.

As increasing knowledge of the universe is discovered by science, a decisive choice has to be made. Is it by chance that everything we know has happened, or was there a first cause? The law of cause and effect prevails across the universe. Indeed, science assures it. By first cause we mean the fundamental source of all being, not just temporal priority. So, was there no first cause for what happened in the Big Bang, some 13.7 billion or more years ago? Some scientists suggest the possibility of a "multiverse," other universes different from our own, from which ours sprang. That only pushes the question of a first cause further back. Are all just by chance, and as this universe constituted with time and space? Believers choose to maintain that a superior mind is the Creator. Science itself throws up even more incredible data than that.

If God as first cause is accepted what support can be adduced? Here the general picture the Bible presents of God is relevant. The emphasis is on the general picture. It is possible to fasten on specific passages that present God in a light thought unacceptable today. Atheists fasten on to them; some believers do not want to face them. It is important in this matter to recognize that if God has revealed himself to human beings it was always within the culture and understanding of their time. We must distinguish truth that is abiding from elements that are reflections of the culture.

In popular religion there are all sorts of views about God. A general tendency is to regard him as an asset, to be used when there is need. God is not our asset. He is our holy Sovereign. He does not exist for us; we ultimately exist for him. Our ultimate well-being and destiny lie in centering our life on him, putting him first.

The general picture given in Scripture is of God as supreme, whose nature is goodness and love. It is theoretically possible that a supreme being could be essentially evil. There is after all much evil in the world we know. But the wonder of the Universe, which operates on laws that scientists perceive as beautiful; and the wonder of our planet's life, even taking account of what we call natural disasters, would appear to rule out an evil power as first cause.

If God is good—the Bible maintains holy and good—and God is love, how are those qualities to be understood? Atheists, incidentally, maintain that goodness and love in God cannot be real, if he is also said to be all-powerful. If he was loving and powerful how could he allow all the evil that does exist in the world? End of argument! The error is to misunderstand the nature of God's love. It is not so much a matter of feelings, an emotional response to what is attractive, but an act of the will to effect the well-being of the beloved at whatever cost to the lover. Further, love wills the beloved to be fulfilled, to act freely. Love does not enforce, compel, manage; it respects the freedom of the loved one.

The love of God—and the free will of the loved one—is seen clearly in creation. The universe he brought into being was allowed to develop, evolve, according to its laws. So it was, and is, by evolution everything has developed. Charles Kingsley, a Christian leader in the nineteenth century, put it this way: God could have made a universe complete; he did something more wonderful, he created a universe that could make itself. Science recognizes that everything is not pre-determined according to some blueprint. There are situations open to different possibilities. In the first moments of the Big Bang, developments could have gone one way, and we would not now be here. They went the other way and we eventually arrived on this planet. In human life, choices are faced in response to different situations. We can go one way or another, and we know the choice is genuine; we are not pre-determined.

The more science discovers about the universe the greater is the wonder and mystery of God if we choose to believe in him. From the moment of the Big Bang when we are told there were only two elements, hydrogen and helium, a multiplicity of atoms evolved. These atoms operate throughout the whole cosmos, reckoned by scientists to be more than twenty-eight billion light years across—a light year being the distance travelled by light in a year, about six million million miles. Atoms are not the smallest thing; activity goes on within each. A Nobel prize-winning physicist, Richard Freyman, said, "All things are made of atoms—little particles that move around in perpetual motion, attracting one another when they are a little distance apart, but repelling upon being squeezed into one another." It is reckoned that each one of us is made up of ten thousand trillion trillion atoms. We are a tiny part of a solar system around a relatively small star, the sun. That system is part of a galaxy containing around a hundred billion stars, the galaxy itself one of at least a hundred billion galaxies. And atoms make up them all. Could there be any more amazing or mind-stunning claim than that God is responsible for all this? Yet many, including scientists, believe it.

In the evolution of this planet with all its good and beneficial developments, there is also what is harmful. Genetic mutation is the source of both new forms of life and of malignancy. Deadly viruses; genetic disorders that cause incurable illnesses; creatures like the parasite in female mosquitoes that causes malaria for millions; cancer—all affect the human race. Some people assess natural disasters as either direct acts of God, presumably in judgment, or as evidence that God does not exist. In fact, life would not have been possible on earth but for natural events such as volcanoes, earthquakes, shifting of tectonic plates. They brought about our atmosphere. It would be inconsistent with God's permitting love to switch off these natural events now we exist, as it would be to withdraw the freewill of human beings because they abuse it to do evil things.

The attempt has been made to indicate it is reasonable to believe in God when his nature is perceived in the Scriptures. But there is a further strand for a convinced believer. It is, in my case, a lifetime's experience of trusting in God and seeking to shape my life on him. This kind of experience is diagnosed by Dawkins and others as an illusion. I regard their claim as unjustifiable arrogance. I would not condemn as an illusion Dawkins's claim that he has moved from an earlier attachment to religion to atheism—I might question the veracity and understanding of what he once believed. Nor would I ever doubt his scientific knowledge. But I refute his claim that all I have experienced over eighty years of life is a deceptive illusion. Since university days I have developed a critical mind, wanting to question and test my own convictions as well as what is presented in books and articles. Indeed in seventeen years of retirement I have critically tested convictions I had built up over previous years. I have now changed my position regarding some things I was once certain of; other convictions I have become more certain of. Since studying psychology at university I have been very aware that persons can choose to believe what they want to believe. There are abundant examples every day in human affairs, not least among adherents of religion. But in the last years of my life I want to be sure of my convictions. Guidance from God when perplexed by life, support through long trials, deliverance from harmful situations, relief of conscience when sin is confessed to God, peace in storms of life, fulfilment in service of God, enabling to use what gifts I have, are all blessings I treasure. I find it impossible to believe that all these benefits arise from my own mind, even its subconscious part. They are gifts of God. And not least among them is the fervent hope of eternal life with God.

3

God's Story

ESSENTIALLY THE Bible presents God's story. It is not there simply to satisfy our curiosity, to add one more story to those that have grown since *Homo sapiens* first imagined another world to which to relate while in this world and to hope for after death. God's story in Scripture draws us to find our salvation in him so that our destiny may be realized.

The story begins with the Creation. God creates not because he needs to out of an incompleteness in himself. In the social relationship of the Trinity—a concept to be explored later—God is complete, perfect. But his love impels him to share his nature with others for their fulfilment and well-being. He loves what he creates. That entails allowing what he loves to develop. So the created universe evolves on the basis of laws perceived by scientists as beautiful. Everything is not pre-determined. Developments arise that present choice of direction. Thus when beings emerge with freedom to act in accord with or contrary to what is good, evil consequences can occur.

The origin of evil has exercised human minds. The Bible's assertions regarding the origin of evil point to the realm of eternity in which spirit beings, angels, have been created to fulfil his purposes. Because God is love, they have been given free will—they are not programmed as robots. In fact, rebellion has come about within their ranks. One, given the name of Lucifer, also referred to as the devil, or Satan, is presented as the chief rebel. The nature of the rebellion is described as pride, which is centering life on the self rather than God. The Bible indicates the devil as aiming to frustrate God's purposes throughout creation, influencing human beings to sin, and supremely to undermine God's decisive act in Christ, his incarnate Son. Some, even in the Christian religion, find difficulty in accepting the idea of angels and of a personal devil. But it can be argued that faced with the prevalence of evil the Bible's story makes sense. Actions of individuals, and even more of regimes, appear so evil that a purely human origin hardly seems adequate.

Continuing with God's story it is clear that he anticipated the entry of sin into the human race, but because of his love for us determined to provide the remedy. That remedy will be to reconcile humans to himself, deal with their sin, and bring them at last to their ultimate goal of perfect harmony with himself and thus to their ultimate well-being. It also means countering the devil's destructive purposes along the way. It is beyond doubt that God must effect all this himself, at whatever cost to himself. He could not leave it to humans to provide the remedy.

How did God set about the task? First, by choosing one people through whom he could bring his saving plan

to all. The primary objective with this chosen race was
to convince his people, and through them, all peoples,
that there is only one God and his ways are good and
essential to human well-being. It was a lesson his people
were very slow to learn. All around were nations given
to polytheism, often associated with degrading practices.
It took over a thousand years to get monotheism established in his people. And though the privileged position
Israel had been given was to be a blessing for all nations,
she selfishly kept it for her own possession. In time God
promised that though Israel had not fulfilled her purpose, another servant would come who would fulfil it.
That servant was to be the Messiah, the one anointed to
achieve God's saving purpose.

The action of saving; redeeming humanity could only
be taken on by God himself. So he became man in Jesus
Christ, thus achieving the action himself within humanity. In the incarnate life of his Son, God revealed himself
more fully than ever before in previous times. Jesus was
able to say, "He who has seen me has seen the Father."
The crucial act of redemption was in the Crucifixion and
Resurrection. Many explanations have been offered to
show how the action of Good Friday and Easter Day ac-
complishes salvation. Some are crude and miss the point.
It was not a case of God in wrath punishing an innocent
third party, Jesus, instead of us. The action of God in the
Cross must be seen as entirely God's in his Trinity, at total
cost to himself. If, as has been emphasized earlier, God is
perfectly good—holy—he must judge evil by separating
it from himself. As light and darkness cannot co-exist, so
neither can God and evil. God's wrath is his implacable

opposition to evil, which destroys his purposes of love and thus robs those he loves of their well-being.

The Cross is judgment by God, borne by God. What that means is difficult for humans to fathom, but perhaps in the Cry of Dereliction uttered by Christ we have a clue. A quotation from Psalm 22, "My God, why have you forsaken me?" points to the element of separation experienced within the Trinity—an eternal perfect relationship this once suffering separation. And yet this separation and judgment made within humanity clears humanity. Once and for all, human sin is judged and removed as a barrier to unity with a holy God. For all who will receive it, God's complete forgiveness is assured. Henceforth human beings are set on track to journey to God's ultimate goal, perfect glory and fulfilment in Heaven. Thus, also, the Devil's main purpose is defeated. The Cross is God's victory over him. The decisive battle has been won. The war will continue to the end of time, but its outcome is finally established. Truly, Jesus Christ, God's Son, reigns from the tree of Calvary. And that victory issues in the Resurrection.

The Resurrection is many things. It is the return to life of Jesus; it is the conquest of physical death for all who trust in him, guaranteeing their ultimate resurrection; it is the confirmation that the sacrifice made by God on Calvary has achieved its purpose; and it is the start of a new creation. The old creation we inhabit is ever changing, subject to decay, from the galaxies of stars to the simplest organisms on this planet. Pain is an inevitable part for animate creatures. It is not unreasonable to believe that for a God who is perfect and eternal this creation does not completely fulfil his purpose. In Christ's Resurrection a new creation begins. It starts in time, as the rising of Christ from the tomb was an event in history, followed by other events over forty days. Like all earlier actions of God, including supremely the Incarnation, it was an intervention of eternity into time. The kingdom of God, also called the kingdom of heaven, proclaimed and manifested by Jesus, is both guaranteed and effected in Christ's Resurrection.

That kingdom, the reign of God's holiness, righteousness, peace, and justice, has become possible and actual now within the present creation. The first three petitions of the prayer Jesus taught his disciples—the hallowing of God's name, meaning the offering of reverence of creature to Creator, the petition for the coming of God's kingdom, and the fulfilment of God's will—are all to be accomplished "on earth as in heaven."

The New Testament indicates that all who respond to God by faith are to be involved in the purposes of God's kingdom, now inaugurated in Christ through his Death and Resurrection. That means proclaiming the good news of God's saving love; working for justice for the oppressed, relief of poverty, care for the needy restoration of the outcasts of society; working for peace. These works were at the heart of Jesus' own ministry until his crucifixion. They had also been what God through his prophets required of his people in Old Testament times. To pray in the Lord's Prayer: "Thy kingdom come on earth as in heaven" must go with commitment to its priorities.

Nevertheless, the perfection of God's new creation and fulfilment of his kingdom can never come within the confines of time. For one thing, those who enter the kingdom remain in this life both sinful and fallible. Though forgiveness is always received as they turn to God in penitent faith, they frequently fail to live up to their status in the new creation. Their baptism reminds them they are to die to sin and rise again into resurrection—a moral possibility because of their incorporation into Christ's Death and Resurrection.

The Scriptures are emphatic that God will complete what he has now begun at the Appearing of Christ. The Appearing, the Parousia of Christ, will bring to an end the present creation and usher in consummation of all God's purposes of love. Time will end, eternity will be all. God's story will be complete, in a new heaven and earth, as the Bible calls it.

This story can be believed. Given that there is a God, supreme and good, and that in his love he does not achieve his purposes by compulsion, but allows humanity freedom of action, his story in Scripture has inner consistency. It demonstrates God's initiative, acting in accord with a plan from the start, and accomplished at his own cost. He calls us to enter his plan and offers his help to fulfil our part. It is a story that could hardly have been imagined by human wish or desire. Even though dreams of a spirit world and life after death have developed over human history, the main features of God's story are not what humans would dream up—the greatest thing God ever did, the death of his Son by cruel execution, and the rising again of his Son in resurrection. Even after death, a martyr's death, humans might imagine a ghost appearance. But they would not imagine a new form of body from which a former leader and friend would relate to them in a loving relationship; the same person but different.

God's story is not just credible to me, among many millions over history from all races and cultures, but it is life changing. It works. In the present post-modern culture there is disinclination to look to absolute systems of belief, to any final authority for belief and behaviour, but to find something that "works for you." So in a supermarket of available systems of self-fulfilment a wide selection is on offer. But God's story has final authority, credibility, and experiential validity. It is possible to know God, not just as an object of speculative thought but embraced in an inner relationship. In the Bible's terms, such knowledge of God is not just a new discovery, but a new birth.

Within the Bible's record of God's story it is clear that he remains a mystery beyond our grasp, as well as one who reveals what we need to know for participation in his saving purposes. Throughout the history of his chosen, servant people, Israel, he is unambiguously revealed as one God. Monotheism is established. But then through the Incarnation more is revealed. The followers of Jesus come to realize slowly that their Master is more than man. Even when they learn to think of him as the Messiah, promised for centuries, that in itself does not convince that he is God, though sent by God. But he speaks of a relationship to the Father, such as no other man had. He accepts their worship. He forgives sins, which as Jews they knew only God could do. Then in the Resurrection he is seen to be "the Son of God with power," to quote Paul's words. Before his crucifixion and final removal of his bodily presence he promises to return and be with them forever. On the day of Pentecost they experience that promise's fulfilment. God is with them, dwelling in them, personally as well as corporately, by his Spirit. Thus they realize the oneness of God is not as simple as they had been brought up to believe; there is a new understanding of God as Trinity, three persons in one relationship. They have to use the human word "persons," though inadequate. The doctrine of the Trinity was born out of the experience of their relationship with him. They have come to know the Father through his Son, Jesus Christ, who was with them by the Holy Spirit. Although articulated later by church councils, the Trinity was experienced before it became a doctrine.

They were, in fact, living in the Trinity before there was need to attempt definition. And, indeed, human beings still today are invited to live in the Trinity while in this life. Being welcomed within the corporate love of the Father, the Son, and the Holy Spirit, they are meant to experience joy, peace, forgiveness, fulfilment, hope. In other words, they are to enjoy what it fully means to be human according to God's purpose in creating them. They thus know, not just with head knowledge, God as Creator, Father, Savior, Brother, Lord, and Indwelling Spirit, personally and corporately.

4

What Will Happen?

THE BIBLE offers truth about the Last Things that must be explored. But before attempting this, questions about the future of this present creation need to be faced. Earth has existed for some four and a half billion years, derived from the sun, a second-generation star, which itself was formed from the stardust of a first generation star. Scientific understanding of the physical laws operating throughout the universe has established that the hydrogen at the core of the sun will be exhausted in about five billion more years. It will become a red giant, burning up all life that remains on this planet, a process that has been observed elsewhere in the cosmos. This is assuming life on our planet has not been wiped out by a collision with another cosmic body such as happened some sixty-five million years ago, and that humanity has not brought about such global warming as makes life impossible. Some scientists have suggested that hope for the survival of humanity may lie with emigration to another part of the universe—a prospect that seems to defy rational expectation.

It is not, however, the future of the sun and its planetary system which has to be faced. What is the future of the universe? From the moment of the Big Bang it has been expanding from that infinitely small start. The expansion element is one of two forces that affect everything. The other element is gravity, which holds matter together. Two possibilities lie before the cosmos in the very distant future. One is that all things will decay into cold death, driven by dark energy. That is, if expansion continues. The other possibility is that expansion will slow down, gravity will predominate, the expansion will be reversed, and the universe will implode. What began with the Big Bang would end in a Big Crunch. The current expectation favored by cosmologists is cold death. Either case leads to futility; that is, if we rely only on science to envisage the future. Christians may believe this will not be the final verdict on the cosmos. They cannot ignore what cosmologists predict, based on known physical laws that operate throughout the universe, but there is other truth to consider.

The Bible clearly envisages action by God the Creator to determine the future, not only for humanity, but for the universe he began. Indeed God is presented as the God of the future, intervening within time to complete his ultimate purpose of consummation in glory in what is described as "a new heaven and earth." Christian believers, quite naturally, think of God as the God of the past, creating, revealing supremely through Christ, and redeeming through his death and Resurrection. They also are conscious of the God of the present, entering their own lives in grace to remake and sanctify them by his Holy Spirit. But God is also the God of the future. As he led his people in the Old Testament, when they were reluctant to follow, so he leads his people in the new covenant to the goal of perfection. The God of grace is the God of hope; a hope that is not mere wishful thinking, but as sure and certain as his own faithful nature.

The climactic event that will mark the completion of God's purposes is the Parousia, the Appearing of his Son often referred to as Christ's Second Coming, completing the saving work of his First Coming. That Appearing is presented in Scripture in apocalyptic language. Inevitably the language and picture are described in terms drawn from human experience in this current world. Differences exist among Christians as to how literally they should interpret the whole picture of the Appearing. But it will be decisive, sudden, probably unexpected by the general range of human awareness, and will usher in the Last Things. Jesus told his disciples no one knows the time of that event except the Father.

The big question is, how does all this biblical hope fit in with scientific speculations about the end of the cosmos, which seem to add up to futility. That projected futility has led some of atheistic persuasion to conclude that the universe has been pointless, having no purpose. A Christian answer to the question just posed is to point to the Bible's truth about creation in the first place. The Genesis account, while not couched in a scientific, literally historic genre, stresses that creation came by the Word of God. God said, "Let it be," and it was. John's Gospel opens by declaring that: "In the beginning was the Word, and the Word was God . . . all things were made by him."

The word of God is the effective expression of the mind and will of God. Human words are the expression of our minds, desires, and will, but do not always effect what we intend. The word of God is always effective. There is much emphasis on that truth in Scripture. "God's word will not return to him void. It will accomplish that to which he sends it," as Isaiah 55:11 affirms.

It is also clear from the New Testament that not only did God create by his Word, but that all things are held in being by the same Word. Everything in the universe, every moment, exists by the effective expression of God's will. Paul speaks of "all things holding together in Christ" (Col 1:7). The Epistle to the Hebrews begins with reference to Christ as not only having created all things as the Word of God but also as "sustaining all things by the word of power" (Heb 1:3). So it is conceivable that as the first moment of creation was by divine, sudden intervention from eternity, so the end of the cosmos could happen in the same way. But that leads on to another question, will the end of the universe just be destruction, a complete finish? There are passages in the Bible that describe the end in fiery terms—"heavens disappearing with a shrill noise, heavenly bodies burning up and being destroyed" (2 Pet 3:16). That sounds like one of the possibilities envisaged by scientists, the Big Crunch. A clue to interpreting this apocalyptic language may be found in a familiar feature of life in the area of Jerusalem in Christ's day. Outside the city was the Valley of Gehenna, the rubbish dump, in which fires burned continually. Corpses of executed criminals were dumped there. The fires of Gehenna symbolized the destruction of what was no longer needed. Something consumed by fire was finished with. To maintain that the vivid fiery references in Scripture fit in with scientific projections about the Big Crunch would appear to present a bigger problem than it solves. The Big Crunch would be billions of years hence, long after this planet had ended and humanity had long ceased to be part of creation. It is true that God seems in our terms to be a patient creator. It is estimated that carbon-based life, on which our existence depends, was only possible after ten billion years, when the chemical context came about. But for the Parousia and the culmination of all God's purposes to be billions of years hence would seem to be inconsistent with all we know of God's relationship with humanity as the Bible's story presents it.

Does God intend to destroy the universe in final extinction? It has been maintained earlier that it was an expression of God's love to create the universe. He takes pleasure in it, and it reflects his glory. Would it not be consistent with these truths if God recycled his creation rather than just wiped it out? Human beings now see the value of recycling rather than destroying. And indeed the nature of the universe itself is to recycle. The elements that make up all life go on to make new life. The dust of dead stars becomes new stars. The chemical elements of all life on this planet pass on to new expressions. God's way is to remake and restore. There is a significant passage regarding this in Romans 8:19–22. There creation is described as groaning with labor pains, awaiting a consummation along with God's people. At present it is subject to decay, but it looks forward to freedom from its slavery to decay.

There is an echo in Old Testament prophetic writings where a glorious, peaceful picture for the earth is offered. Obviously, we have no idea what God will do in fulfilling his purpose for the universe. But the pattern of birth, life, decay, and death will no longer apply. The Scripture is content to speak of a new heavens and earth. Presumably, the physical laws that govern everything in the cosmos will no longer operate. Discontinuity with the present universe is beyond doubt. What continuity will mean, we cannot know.

In all the speculations that inevitably arise from scientific projections into the future, and in the truths that meet us in Scripture, the overriding fact for Christians is that God, who in love created all things and has intervened in time to save humanity, is going to complete his purposes in a future of glory. He can never be anything but faithful. And the key to all his purpose is the Resurrection of Christ.

5

The Resurrection of Christ

THE WAY that Christ's Resurrection determines and shapes the future will be considered in all that later follows. It therefore requires closer study now. Did it really happen? Some scholars cast doubt on the New Testament narratives, suggesting that Jesus' spirit survived death and appeared to them in visions, but his body remained dead. And then to make the story of the early church more convincing, Jesus' followers embroidered their experiences with the accounts we now read. There is no doubt that most Jews, but not all, believed in life after death and looked forward to some future resurrection. But a careful and open-minded reading of the text indicates that the first disciples believed they were confronted with something quite different from their former beliefs inherited through the Jewish faith. We may clearly recognize differences in detail in the Gospel accounts and at the beginning of the Acts of the Apostles. But accounts of the same events presented by different persons will always present different features, according to what strikes the individual. And when—as in the case of these several accounts—they have been at first passed on by oral tradition, differences will be remembered.

Some critics direct attention to the empty tomb. Though emphasized in the Gospels, it is stressed that neither Paul nor other letter writers refer to an empty tomb. But that need have no significance. The epistle writers knew the earlier accounts, and what was important to them was not an empty tomb but the significance of a risen Christ.

What can be said about the accounts of the first Easter day? First, that no early visitors to the tomb expected it to be empty. The women came to anoint a dead body, and could not understand what had happened to it. Mary Magdalene thought someone had taken the corpse away. The Roman guard and Jewish leaders, fearing what Jesus' friends would make of the situation, concocted a story that the body had been stolen. The disciples did not immediately grasp the truth about the Resurrection. Indeed even during the forty days after that first Easter some needed a lot of convincing. Even at the final appearance of the risen Christ at his ascension, we read that some still doubted, indicating they did not know what to make of the Resurrection.

What did bring conviction? First, there were many persons of different character, intelligence, and trustworthiness who had been present at Christ's appearances. Some time before the first Gospel was compiled (probably by Mark relying heavily on Peter), Paul calls attention to these eyewitnesses in 1 Corinthians 15:6, as he introduces his major chapter on the Resurrection. He reminds his readers that Jesus appeared after his Resurrection to Peter, James, and all the apostles and, further, to about five hundred people at once. And, he continues, most of this crowd were still alive at the time of his writing. No one would allow that claim to go unchallenged if it were not true.

Further conviction came from experience of a tremendous change that came over their lives. Before his crucifixion, the disciples dreaded the departure Jesus told them about. Their hopes had been that he would restore the fortunes of their nation. And his forecast of his ministry ending in violent death caused them to try to deter him from going to Jerusalem. When the Crucifixion happened, they were devastated. It took time for them to accept that Jesus had indeed risen from the dead. Thomas was not alone in doubting the evidence, even when his colleagues insisted it was true. Then, as Jesus had promised before his death, the Holy Spirit came upon them in a dramatic, overwhelming experience on the day of Pentecost, and their lives were transformed. They remembered that Jesus had said it was better for him to withdraw his bodily presence, because he would come back to them by his Spirit. A Christ within them corporately and personally was better than Christ alongside as a companion. Most of them ran away from the cross. But afterwards, they were ready to die for the Christ now within them. Peter had been so scared, he denied three times that he had ever known Jesus. Later he accepted martyrdom.

If Christ had not risen from the dead, the church would never have been born. And it would not have spread throughout the whole world and continued now for over two thousand years. What Jesus had done before his crucifixion would have remained just a movement— among many others in the nation of Israel—that collapsed and would be now long-forgotten. Critics who maintain the Resurrection could not happen, because miracles cannot happen, can offer no convincing explanation as to why the church has survived and won many millions of members over the centuries. Other world religions have founders who are remembered with awe, but they are all dead. No other religion is founded upon faith in a person claimed to be God in humanity who suffered a criminal's execution and rose again to endless life.

The appearances of Jesus as risen presented to his disciples some strange features. He was not always immediately recognized, and only so when he chose to be. Yet before the cross, he was very well known. After his Resurrection, he could suddenly appear and then disappear. He walked and talked to two friends on their way home from Jerusalem, and was invited into their home as if a stranger. It was only as he broke bread with them then that they knew him. Was it by the wound prints on his hands? If so, that is how he established recognition to the disciples on the evening of the first Easter. And it was the sight of his wounds that convinced Thomas a week later. The first reaction of some was that they were seeing a ghost—presumably because of his sudden appearance and disappearance. How did he counteract that? By asking to share food with them. This could only be as a concession to their difficulty in grasping the reality of his person, alive with them. Whatever else we must say about his risen body, it was not subject to digestive process, blood circulation, lungs taking in oxygen. There were no cells dying and being replaced. So it is important to emphasise that for him it was not a matter of bringing dead flesh back to life, but of having a transformed body. Unless he had appeared to them in a recognizable body the truth of the Resurrection would have missed them. He spoke to them, indeed he taught them many truths over forty days. He showed his love to them. He served them; in fact making breakfast for some of them on the shore of Lake Galilee, after some of them had had a fruitless night of fishing. That must have been a stark reminder of when they were first called to be his disciples, when he too helped them with a miraculous catch of fish. On his last appearance of ascension he commissioned them afresh for the work to which he had called them.

The significant features of his risen body will need to be considered when thinking about our own resurrection body and life in heaven. But the underlying factor in all the disciples witnessed was continuity and discontinuity—a phrase that runs through all matters to do with eschatology, the future purposes of God. Undoubtedly Jesus risen was the same person they had been with for three years. He was the same person they had seen nailed to the cross. The relationship of love still obtained. But, as indicated above, there was discontinuity. His body was fundamentally transformed. And after forty days there was no further bodily presence but a continuing and more wonderful presence by his Spirit, promised to the end of time.

What then did the Resurrection of Jesus mean; what did God achieve by raising him? It demonstrated and guaranteed the resurrection of all God's people. Over the centuries before, humanity had looked forward to some existence after death. In Judaism a shadowy existence after death with the hope eventually of some sort of resurrection had captured minds. Jesus' Resurrection is God's incontrovertible promise of our resurrection, and God is faithful to the end and cannot lie.

Furthermore the Resurrection is God's confirmation that his saving sacrifice made on the cross was totally effective. God, the Trinity of Father, Son, and Holy Spirit, judged sin and removed its curse entirely at his own cost, defeated all the forces of evil, so that their final elimination is assured, thus revealing that his love for humanity is infinite. We may ask, how might we know that the Atonement of Calvary was effective if Jesus had not risen? The Resurrection of Jesus opened the way for his risen life and power to be available for his church through all time and for each individual believer. We do not look back into distant history to a dead leader, a great teacher, an inspiring hero long gone. He is with us now bringing the life of God by his Spirit.

However, wider in significance than what the Resurrection means to believers—to the church throughout all time—is the fact that God's new creation was established on that first Easter. God had created the present creation in love—had, we believe, delighted in it and had related directly with self-conscious, God-conscious humanity.

But by its very nature the old creation is subject to decay, death and pain. God's interventions from eternity into history pointed to a better, perfect future. And in Jesus, God made clear his kingdom was entering the realm of time. "The Kingdom of Heaven is at hand" was an oft-repeated message of Jesus. It was present in him, and was established in his resurrection. Again, it has to be emphasized; the principle of continuity and discontinuity applies.

Another way of describing the new creation is as the Kingdom of Heaven. Entering this world in the person of the incarnate Son, the kingdom continues to grow in the mission established after the Resurrection. In the life and work of the church and wherever God's rule is operating, the kingdom expands. The growth is silent, that is, often unrecognized by the world around.

But the church is the sign of the kingdom. It must exhibit its characteristics—righteousness, justice, holiness, peace and love. It is also the instrument by which those qualities are fulfilled. And it is the foretaste of what the kingdom will be in its fullness. So, Jesus taught his disciples to pray: "Your kingdom come." The Resurrection is the guarantee it will.

The manifestation of Christ's risen body may provide the clue to address a question raised in the previous section on the fate of the universe. Will it end in extinction, or be recycled into a new and permanent existence? The suggestion there made was that God's love for his creation could lead to a renewed existence no longer subject to decay and death. Continuity and discontinuity in Jesus Christ from life before death to life after his resurrection could anticipate the universe's future in God's new creation. The truth that with the Resurrection of Christ the new creation is assured and begun must not be underestimated.

6

Death

DEATH IS the first of the Last Things to be considered. It is, of course, what meets us first, though it is described as man's last enemy. Though we know it is inevitable, as it is for everything else in the universe, it can for most people present fear. It is fear of how death may overtake us that predominates. Will it be a peaceful end, or one of prolonged pain; will it come suddenly early? And such pleasure we enjoy in this life, particularly in relationships, we dread losing. The death of those we love brings great sorrow.

It is apparent that writers of the New Testament documents attributed physical death to the fact that we are fallen humanity. They took the story in Genesis 3 as literal history. They could not be expected to know differently. It is still right for us in modern times to attribute spiritual death—that is, separation from a holy God—to sin. And the Genesis story can be taken as teaching that spiritual truth.

Mortality is universal, but is it not true that human beings are immortal? Different convictions are held among Christians, attempting to understand the Scriptures correctly. There are Scriptures that suggest all humans are unconditionally immortal, that all will continue throughout eternity with God or apart from God, in heaven or hell. Other Scriptures may be taken to reveal that humans are not inherently immortal, that not all born into the world will have life eternally. Indeed, it can be said that all have sinned and thus do not have immortality as of right. Eternal life must be received from God or it is not ours: "the wages of sin is death [in the sense of being cut off from God] but the gift of God is eternal life" (Rom 6:23). Jesus and his apostles describe the receiving of eternal life as a new birth, as radical as our natural birth. This is not to deny God made humanity for eternity, nor that he has planted eternity in our hearts, that is, to desire it. But eternal life, a richer concept than mere immortality, is granted by God's direct action in the soul.

In a human being, that which relates to God is sometimes described as spirit, and other times as soul. The soul can be understood as the unique personality that develops from birth and goes on throughout life. It is shaped by our genes, experiences, relationships, and choices. If the foregoing is a right understanding of the gift of eternal life, spirit may be understood as that new life which relates to God. According to Genesis God made humanity in his own image; this includes a capacity to relate to him. If this capacity is lost by humanity's sin, it follows that it is restored by the regenerating work of the Holy Spirit, a work signified and pledged in baptism.

What happens at death? Clearly the body disintegrates either in earth or sea, or in the fires of cremation. Whatever the Resurrection will accomplish, it will not be a reassembling of the flesh and bones of the body the soul has inhabited. If, as the Bible insists, there is a Day of Judgment to come, then it is reasonable to assume that the soul is held in the memory of God. The limitation of our human knowledge is apparent in this matter, but we can rest on the infinity of God's continuing knowledge. If the spirit represents the relationship established by the grace of God it will go, as we may say, to its home in God. In Colossians 3:3, Paul used a phrase to describe the present life of those who trust in God: "Your life is hid with Christ in God." If that is true in life here, it must be all the more true after the death of the believer. There is much evidence in Scripture to support that the state of the believer's soul after death is to be at rest, in peace with God.

A relevant question arises about communication with those departed in relationship with God. Sentiment on the part of those left behind in this life and bereaved leads to the wish, even hope, to be able to make contact. Despite an age-long interest in mediums and séances the Bible warns against any attempt to contact the departed. Whatever claims are made it is well to remember that all people are inclined to believe what they want to believe. The same charge can be made against Christian believers, but they will hold on to God's revelation in history and supremely in Jesus Christ. The faithfulness of God is the bedrock of their faith.

Are the departed in Christ able to know what is going on in the lives of their loved ones who remain on earth? Again, sentiment, or wishful thinking, inclines some to think so. However, if the departed are at rest, that peace would certainly be disturbed or undermined by knowing our pains, sorrows, fears, sins, tragedies. "May they rest in peace" is a prayer that should meet the needs of the living.

Over centuries, in the Catholic tradition of the church, the belief grew that the living could pray to saints who were departed, particularly to the Virgin Mary. There is no justification in the New Testament for this belief and practice. Indeed, it is emphasized that we have one and only mediator with God, the Ascended Christ. He is presented in the Epistle to the Hebrews and elsewhere as our great High Priest who has entered into God's presence as our Intercessor. We have no need of any saints to present our prayers to God. The Ascended Christ pleads our cause, not by petitions but by his presence. We are baptized into Christ and so may approach the throne of God with confidence. The Epistle to the Hebrews maintains that Christ has entered once for all into God's presence on the basis of his own sacrifice for sins forever. This is in contrast to the work of the High Priest in the Old Testament system, entering the most holy presence of God each year to repeat sacrifices. In defense of the invocation of saints, the Roman doctrine appeals to tradition, the accumulated wisdom of the church. While tradition and reason have a part to play in the interpretation of Scripture, it is Scripture that must govern tradition.

Does the Communion of Saints, an article in the creeds, and consonant with Scripture, alter the position maintained above? Does the fact that the church on earth is one with the church in Heaven open up the possibility that we now may contact those in Heaven? Again, the New Testament would give no support to that. In the Eucharist we declare that we are offering our sacrifice of praise and thanksgiving along with the angels and company of Heaven, and the Sacrament affirms that and points to us being entirely one at last "when Jesus comes." But we should be content with Christ as Lord being the one who unites us now. And it is particularly appropriate at the Eucharist to give thanks for the blessings received from God through our departed loved ones, for their present rest in his presence, and the glorious hope of resurrection and reunion at the return of Christ. There is an assuring statement quoted a hundred years ago by one of the greatest theologians in Britain in modern times, P. T. Forsyth, in his book, *This Life and the Next*: "I know that land. Some of my people live there. Some have gone abroad there on secret foreign service, which does not admit of communications. But I meet from time to time the Commanding Officer. And when I mention them to Him He assures me all is well." Whether the departed are still able to pray to God for us, as they did in life, we may leave that to God.

What can be said to Christian believers as they contemplate their own death? There is no promise in Scripture that death will mentally be peaceful or painless. We remember those who have faced a martyr's death. There is no promise that death will come only in ripe old age, that fatal illnesses will be avoided. What is promised is the presence of Christ, with inner strength and transference to Heaven. "Though I walk through the valley of the shadow of death. I will fear no evil, for You are with me" (Ps 23:4). An old lady left this verse behind her:

> Since Jesus is mine; I will not fear undressing
> But gladly leave off this garment of clay
> To die in the Lord is a Covenant blessing
> Since Jesus my Savior through death led the way.

7

Judgment

"I T IS appointed unto man once to die and after that
the Judgment," says Hebrews 9:27. Among people
who have not rejected the idea of God, an ambiguous
attitude toward a Day of Judgment prevails. There is a
basic feeling that in the end, evil things done by nations
and individuals ought to be punished. Just as there is a
general acceptance of punishment for crime in societies
claiming to be civilized, so if there is a God sustaining the
moral order wickedness must get its due deserts. On the
other hand, the same people hope that any judgment for
them will be very lenient, making generous allowances.
This reflects their attitude to the way they hope justice
will operate in their own society. Crimes like murder or
grievous bodily harm must be taken seriously, but they
hope to evade judgment for their own speeding offenses,
parking in prohibited areas, tax evasion, and the like.
In other words, they create self-assessed gradations of
justice that operate for their own benefit. The same approach relates to any Judgment Day.

Any minister of religion visiting a bereaved family prior to a funeral may be told the departed was a wonderful person, that he or she never did anyone any harm. The inference is, apparently, that they must be all right with God; no judgment really expected, a passport straight through to heaven.

But what is the truth the Bible presents? That God is the just judge and that all humanity will appear before him at the last. In all recognition that God is indeed love, unending, self-giving love, there must be emphasis on his holiness.

He is perfect goodness, purity, and light, and no evil can continue in his presence. "God is Light, and in him is no darkness at all," says John (1 John 1:5). The judgment of God must banish evil from his presence. We are reminded in the teaching of Jesus that evil is not just a matter of acts but of thoughts and attitudes. And again John says, "If we say we have no sin, we deceive ourselves, and the truth is not in us" (1 John 1:8).

Unless, therefore, the creation is a totally amoral system, with no test of right or wrong, there must be final judgment. The Bible presents that as a consequence upon the Appearing of Christ. While Christ maintained that he did not come into the world to carry out that judgment, it is clear that it is through him that the final judgment will be exercised. Paul told the Athenian debaters, "God has appointed a day in which he will judge the world by that Man he has chosen" (Acts 17:31). This leads us to the truth that judgment is exercised by reference to relationship with Christ. There are instances in his teaching that indicate simply his presence among the people of his day was beginning the work of conviction, and after he left the earth his Holy Spirit would carry on this work. He would convict persons about sin, evil, because of their lack of belief in Christ. The implication is clear. Their sin could be dealt with through faith in Christ.

The third of the three tasks of the Holy Spirit in John 16:8–11 will be to show people they have a wrong idea of judgment. What Jesus adds then sounds strange—he goes on to say that their idea of judgment is wrong because the ruler of this world has already been judged. The devil, the origin of all evil according to the Bible, stands under God's judgment. This may refer to his exclusion from God's kingdom because of his rebellion in pride, but also may connect with what Christ was to achieve through the cross. There the decisive defeat of the devil and all evil would be effected so that final destruction of evil would ensue.

These insights inevitably lead us to the cross and its role in judgment. No presentation of the Christian faith can be adequate unless it is recognized that the Death and Resurrection of Jesus was the greatest thing God ever did. Some may regard Jesus as the greatest prophet God ever sent. Others will go further and see his incarnate life as showing us what God is like. Further, it may well be said that in the cross God shows us how much he loves us, and that he is always with us in our sufferings. But the New Testament will not let us stop there. In the sacrifice of Calvary God dealt finally and totally with sin, with all evil. And what God did was entirely at cost to himself. Different human categories have been applied to what was done on the cross—punishment, penalty, substitution. They struggle to get to the heart of the matter, which we may say is God judging evil once and for all. This was accomplished within humanity, in that Jesus was truly man, but the Trinity—Father, Son, and Holy Spirit—paid the price. And this price was paid to God's holy and just rule.

It has been emphasized that evil must be judged by separation, by alienation, or banishment from God's presence. At the heart of the cross, then, was a separation borne by God. Do we not have a glimpse into this in the Cry of Dereliction, "My God, my God, why have you forsaken me?" (taken from Psalm 22). What that entailed, humans can never really know, but does it not mean that the perfect harmony and unity shared within the Trinity was severed in the act of judgment? Not by letting sinners off, not by implying it doesn't really matter, not even by just saying, "I forgive you," but by an infinitely costly act of God himself could evil be judged and put away. If God in his overall purposes became one of us in the person of his Son, and all to lead up to the awful death as of a criminal in crucifixion, the necessity for such an action must be absolute. As has already been mentioned, it was not only human evil that was dealt with, but the devil and all his forces were decisively beaten. So, if we rightly claim that through the cross God's saving act was accomplished, it was therefore done by grace through judgment.

It is the cross and Resurrection of the incarnate God that makes the Christian faith unique among all religions. Humans would never imagine a God who submits himself to the rejection, injustice, cruelty, and agony of crucifixion, and all to suffer the consequences of human evil in order to save and restore humanity to himself. And all this is completed in resurrection from death into transformed life. But God did it and revealed its truth to his chosen servants.

It would be presumptuous to attempt to decide how God will choose to judge on that last day. Jesus made different points in his teaching. He spoke of nations being judged. He foretold judgment on those failing to relieve the needs of folk in distressing circumstances: prison, poverty, hunger, sickness. These could be seen as failure to keep the two great commandments, love for God and for neighbor. The general theme of the New Testament, however, is that the crucial issue in judgment will be faith in God. Some would insist on restricting the definition of faith to a conscious trust in Christ in his Death and Resurrection. That insistence prompts two questions. What of those who lived before Christ, and could not anticipate the meaning of his Death and Resurrection taught by the apostles after the events? We may be justified in claiming the issue will be their trust in God according to the light they had in their time. Secondly, what of those after the Incarnation who belong to other faiths? Will they be judged according to the light they have had? To all speculation the answer must be: "shall not the Judge of all the earth do right?"—an answer that dates back to Abraham (Gen 18:25).

To all who are cleared on the Day of Judgment, the basis will be what God himself has done through Christ in the cross and Resurrection. Its efficacy covers the past, the present, and the future. It is retrospective for all time before Christ and prospective for all the future.

Jesus came "that the world through him might be saved." The saving work was for all humanity. It is the mission of the Christian church to call all to a personal faith in Christ as Savior, but in the end they must leave the judgment to God.

There is another aspect of the judgment raised in the New Testament. It is the assessment of the service rendered by believers during their earthly life. And in this the element of reward is relevant. In 1 Corinthians 3, Paul speaks of Christian service built on the foundation of faith in Christ. Some build with gold, silver, precious stones. Others build with wood, grass, or straw. As fire would test the value and durability of these different substances, so Judgment Day will reveal the quality of the life and service of believers. Paul makes plain it is not the eternal destiny of any that will be at issue, but rather the possibility or otherwise of reward. What the nature of reward will be is not for us to know now, but the principle of reward is consistent with a just God.

8

Hell

THE DAY of Judgment leads to two destinies, heaven and hell. The Bible has much to say about both. The English word, hell, covers a number of different concepts and terms used in the Hebrew and Greek of the writings. In the Old Testament, Hades, or Sheol, is the abode of the departed spirits. It is a shadowy realm, a waiting room before some final action of God that will establish a paradise of blessing. For some Jews, this concept would entail resurrection. The Psalmist could speak of "his flesh resting in hope" (Ps 16:9). In the time of Jesus the Pharisees believed in a resurrection, the Sadducees did not. The creeds speak of Jesus at his death "descending into hell," the place of departed spirits.

In Luke 16:19–31, Jesus told a parable involving Hades. A rich man, Dives, who had done nothing to relieve the poverty and distress of Lazarus, who begged at his gate, found himself in Hades enduring torment. Lazarus is described as being "in Abraham's bosom," a state in which he is blessed. Dives begs that someone go from that place to warn his brothers to change their manner of life, lest they land up where he is. He is told that if the brothers do not now take heed of the Law and the Prophets, they will not be persuaded even by someone rising from the dead. It is vital that we bear in mind a principle that applies to parables in the New Testament. Every part of the story does not have the same theological significance. There is a main point to get at. In this parable, the point is that God's revealed will must be followed in this life. Loving him and loving neighbor, especially when in need, sums up the Law and the Prophets. So, the parable is not to be pressed in order to speculate about the geography of Hades. The great gulf said to exist between Dives and Lazarus may be interpreted to indicate different ultimate destinations. Dives's torment may point to bitter remorse at lost opportunity to do differently.

More often in the teaching of Jesus, hell is spoken of as a final destiny at Judgment Day. Very graphic images—fire, bitter lament, torment—are associated with hell. The general message is to act now so that we avoid that fate. Two points need to be noted. As with all truth about eternity, heaven, and hell, the only language we have is of this world, which can only hint at the truth. Secondly, the pictures of hell relate frequently to a feature of life well known to Jews, particularly in the area of Jerusalem. As has already been mentioned, the Valley of Hinnom, or Gehenna, was the rubbish dump of the city where fires burned consistently destroying the rubbish. Corpses of executed criminals were dumped there. There could not be a more frightening picture of hell. What may be deduced from all references to hell in the New Testament?

First, that it is a reality to be faced on the Day of Judgment. Jesus who came into the world to reveal God more fully than ever before would not have warned so urgently about it if it was not a future reality. A second, incontrovertible fact is that nothing evil can exist in God's holy presence. There could be no glorious consummation of God's loving purposes with evil present. It was the emergence of evil in his first creation that caused such terrible consequences. The new creation of heaven cannot be allowed to be so affected by the presence of evil.

It has already been maintained that the essential nature of God's judgment of evil is to separate it from himself. If heaven is with God, hell must be away from God, and thus it must cease to exist, since everything that exists does so by God's allowance. If that is withdrawn, existence ends.

Does this mean, then, that hell will not exist forever? Here, we must admit, we are faced with no absolute answer. There are many references that suggest a continuing state. There are indications that the devil and all his forces will be cast into hell. But does that indicate extinction? For human beings, the question of immortality is predominant. The position already taken in this book is that human beings are not inherently immortal. The gift of immortality, or eternal life, is given by God in response to faith. "The wages of sin is death, but the gift of God is eternal life," says Paul (Rom 6:23). That gift is directly related to the work of Christ. The writings of John, both in his Gospel and Epistles, make abundantly clear that "eternal life is to know God and Jesus Christ whom he hath sent." A summary can be taken from 1 John 5:11: "God has given us eternal life, and this life is in his Son.

Whoever has the Son has this life." Thus, it appears to be justified to speak of conditional immortality, that is, immortality in eternity being conditional upon faith.

The crucial issue on the Day of Judgment will be faith in God and the basis of acceptance what Christ has done in salvation through his death and Resurrection. How those who have not had opportunity to make a conscious response to Christ—in Old Testament times or since—will be regarded by God is something we can leave to his wisdom and love.

It has been argued by some Christians that there could not be a perfect heavenly state for a God of love if a continuing hell of remorse for some of his creatures remained. Again, speculation may be idle, but if conditional immortality is the truth, it may carry the answer.

A further question arises. Will there be any second chance for those who have had the opportunity to trust in God and never taken it in this life? There appears to be nothing in the Bible to offer that possibility. Individuals may encounter various opportunities in this life, before a final decision. Will a God of love offer a choice after death? We must say we cannot bank on it.

What helped to precipitate the Reformation in the sixteenth century was the medieval church's practice of encouraging bereaved relatives to offer money for masses to be said for the departed. The intention of the bereaved was to ensure the departed would be put right with God. Needless to say, there was no justification for the practice in the New Testament. The urgency, then, for all who hope for a life to come, is to respond to God's offer of saving grace.

9

Heaven

A S WE attempt to speak about heaven as the Bible guides us, it is vital to emphasize that we are not conceiving it just as a place to go to when we die. It has been maintained that Scripture speaks of God's ultimate purpose being a new heaven and earth. There is a future in his eternal plan for a transformed cosmos as well as personal fulfilment for individual souls.

All creation is to be transformed into the new creation, a creation already begun with the Resurrection of Jesus Christ, a new creation we are called to live and share in now. Let us not confine our understanding of heaven to only a hope for ourselves after death. In all that follows on the subject of heaven we recognise the totality of God's purpose for a new heaven and earth. Here I express my debt to a great book by the former bishop of Durham, N. T. Wright, entitled *Surprised by Hope*, referred to in the last section of this book.

Heaven is ours to know and experience now. In all our contacts with our Savior God, we are in touch with heaven in worship, prayer, sacraments, informed Bible study, moments of joy and of crisis.

So, heaven, what will it be like? Anyone who thinks heaven is a possibility, or even more, hopes to be there, is bound to ask that question. Only being able to use the language of this world and familiar categories means descriptions in Scripture need careful interpretation. The tendency to expect what we want must be resisted. Some Muslim men, apparently, are looking forward to being supplied with a group of wives. Some Christians are expecting only to be joined by those who have accepted their way of getting there. The book of Revelation, based on visions given to John on the isle of Patmos, presents the most comprehensive description we have of heaven. Much of the book, however, refers to the history that lay before the Christian believers to whom it was written. They were facing persecution, some martyrdom, their faith in God's purposes severely tested. The book assures them that the victory of God is certain. Their Lord and Savior is the Lord of history. He is presented as the Alpha and the Omega, the first and the last, the one who has conquered death and is ruler over the kings of the earth.

It is not only as the Potentate of Time that Jesus Christ is presented. The book looks forward to the Appearing of Christ to wind up the scroll of time and usher in the final kingdom in heaven. As in other Epistles, that coming is described in vivid terms. It occurs on the clouds of heaven, seen by all, including those who rejected Christ on earth. It is a sudden appearing. Some Christians take these descriptions quite literally. Christ's return in the clouds resembles Jesus' last appearance in this world. In his ascension, a cloud took him from the sight of his disciples, and angels said: "He will return in like manner." In the Bible, the cloud is used as a symbol of God's presence as, for instance, at Sinai and at the Transfiguration. And some devout Jews, still awaiting their Messiah, are expecting a literal entry into Jerusalem. It would appear unwise, however, to interpret literally the apocalyptic language concerning the future. There is fascination in foretelling dramatic future events. A massive battle, Armageddon, between the forces of evil and good, a literal thousand-year reign of Christ on earth, are enthusiastically expected. How on earth human beings could live a thousand years, presumably while vegetation and other creatures remained subject to ordinary life cycle, is not explained. Would no other humans be born? These speculations present difficulties. Regardless of how the apocalyptic descriptions will occur, we must surely be content to believe the Appearance of Christ will be sudden, decisive, and the culmination of all God's purposes.

The pictures of heaven are all of perfection, glory, harmony, and peace. The dimensions of the city John saw are of completeness. Gold, silver, and precious stones constitute its buildings. There is a crystal clear river, but no more sea. That latter point was attractive to me while I had to serve for four years in the Navy in war! But on a serious note, while the sea is restless, subject to storms and can be dangerous, a clear river suggests refreshment, calm, and pleasure.

What can be taken as perfect truth is the complete absence of death, grief, sorrow, and pain. It is vital here to recall the nature of Christ's resurrection appearances.

Compared with his life before his death there was both continuity and discontinuity. He was the same person following the resurrection, but there was a major difference. Mention has been made of what will not continue from this life. What will continue? Relationships, joy, beauty, music, and song, we must surely expect.

The most notable factor in all the visions of heaven is the throne of God and of the Lamb. The Lamb is described as bearing the scars of death. The God who created all things, and who redeemed humanity from the ruin of sin by sacrificial death on the cross, is central to the heavenly kingdom. Worship of all beings in heaven is given to him who is eternal and who has redeemed us by his death.

The church is presented as the Bride of Christ. Made perfect she is joined to Christ forever. The Marriage Supper of the Lamb is the description of that coming together of the church with her Lord. The element of enjoyment and feasting should be noted. Christians anticipate this union with joy every time they celebrate the Eucharist. The sacrament is not only the memorial of the past sacrifice on Calvary; the looking up to the Ascended Christ for renewal by his life of purity, purpose, and power; and the rite by which the church is identified as the Body of Christ. It is also a foretaste, an earnest, of the Marriage Supper of the Lamb. We do it always, until he comes.

So far heaven has been described in the future tense. But heaven is also to be experienced now. All who are baptized into Christ and in a relationship of faith are to be in touch with heaven while living on earth. If, as Paul says, "Your life is hid with Christ in God" (Colossians 3:3), it means living in the Trinity now. The relationship within the Trinity welcomes and includes believers. Heaven, the realm of God, is our home now. The phrase, heaven on earth, can be used loosely to describe an enjoyable experience. But it is what the believer is expected to know, when personally or corporately with others, we relate to God. John in his Revelation was under the control of the Holy Spirit, he says, and saw an open door into heaven. In Christian worship and in personal contact with God we pass through that open door. Two worlds are ours. The more we live in that other world, heaven, the better we will be ready for it one day, and the stronger will be the faith and hope of our final destiny.

It has been emphasized that the Appearing of Christ will usher in the consummation of God's final goal. And the basis and guarantee of the goal, the new creation, is the Resurrection of Christ. What does his Resurrection tell us about God's plan for us? Clearly, we will be raised to eternal life. In the interim after death the soul, or essential personality, is with God. Some find it helpful to think of it being held in God's memory. Our resurrection must mean the soul being united with a body. Human beings are psychosomatic creatures and are only complete when in a body. For the vast majority of those who will be resurrected, the physical body has dissolved entirely into chemical elements lost in the ground, sea, or evaporated in flames. There will be no reassembling of that body. Paul in 1 Corinthians 15—his famous chapter on the resurrection—speaks of us receiving a spiritual body. That must be a vehicle of our spirit made perfect and fit for the heavenly realm.

The question arises, however, how much does the appearance of Christ to his disciples after the Resurrection help us to anticipate our resurrected lives? He appeared as a recognized human being. He did not reveal his identity until he chose to do so. But his form was entirely human: head, torso, limbs. And in his body were the marks of his death wounds. He spoke in the language his friends knew, and partook of food. We must recognize that he could only have convinced them he was the same person and truly alive if he did appear in this way. They had to see it was not the appearance of a ghost. And there had to be a tomb empty of a corpse. So, what can be deduced about our resurrected bodies? It has already been emphasised that discontinuity and continuity applied to Christ's risen body. What of us? Continuity for us will surely relate to our souls, to our unique personality. It would seem highly unlikely that our spiritual body would be a replica of our earthly body. Arms, legs, torso, internal organs, our whole life system now would no longer be needed. Our present body shares the same kind of pattern as other creatures with DNA, genes, and hormones, inherited in the process of evolution that governs everything in the universe. We have only to ask the question, "What age would we want to be resurrected at?" to realize discontinuity with our present body. We might be tempted to hope it would be when in our prime. But anyone in old age knows they are not just the same as decades before. Personality can be richer, more fully developed than earlier in life. And, there is the fact that the some have died very early in life, even as infants. We must expect something different from resurrected bodies. Will God enable such souls to reach their potential? All these speculations, inevitably pointless, serve to underline the discontinuity between now and then. Continuity will relate to the soul, and according to the New Testament that will require a body of some sort, sharing the nature of Christ's resurrection body but without those temporarily necessary features to help the disciples to know him.

It is important in this matter to emphasise the nature of personality. Each person is unique. While sharing almost 100 percent of elements with all other humans, everyone is distinctly different. There is a point in development when they become persons. Some, including the Roman Catholic Church, say it is at the moment of conception. But there are incontrovertible arguments against that. What there is from conception is a bundle of cells, at first smaller than a pinhead. It is human life, with potentiality for personhood. But, many such bundles of cells abort naturally without the mother knowing of their existence. We cannot speak of these as actual persons. It would be incredible to think of God resurrecting these. We cannot say precisely when there is a human person, but it must be when separate existence is possible. The debate about limits on abortion centers on this point. Whatever God's purpose will be for an embryo not surviving after separate existence is possible, with a stillborn, for instance, we cannot say. But it would be unwise to base speculation on wishful thinking.

What will happen to our gender identification in heaven? Gender determines our whole life on earth. Will there be male and female in resurrection bodies? Two highly significant verses in the Bible may help reflection.

Genesis 1:27 indicates that God in creating humanity made male and female "in his own image." Whatever way *Homo sapiens* emerged as a species of creation among others, at some point God brought the creature he loved not only to self-consciousness but also to God-consciousness. Human beings became capable of relating to God with capacity to love, trust and obey, or refuse. The stories in the early chapters of Genesis convey these theological truths. It is important to note that both male and female relate to God and represent him in the world. Genesis 3 tells of the fall of humanity, choosing our own way rather than God's. One consequence of the Fall is a fracturing of relationship between male and female. Instead of the picture of complementary partnership and harmony described in Genesis 2, we have male domination and female submission, some of the worst features still evident in our own day, in spite of greater emancipation of women in many spheres and cultures.

We turn then to the second test of utmost significance for heaven. In Galatians 3:28 Paul declares, "in Christ there is neither Jew nor Gentile, bond nor free, male nor female." In other words, in the new creation inaugurated in Christ distinctions of race, class, and gender no longer apply. Of course, while we are in this life they are not removed, but in the kingdom of God they are irrelevant. We may say that the purpose of God in creating male and female in his own image, marred by the Fall into sin, is restored and becomes effective. Because the church now is the sign, instrument and foretaste of the kingdom the change should be reflected in its life. It is for that reason an increasing number of Christians support the full integration of women in the ordained ministry of the church. Both male and female represent God, each contributing in partnership their gifts and insights. On the basis of this reasoning it is right to look for full integration in heaven. As our personalities or souls are governed so much by our gender now the factor may still be relevant in heaven, although the resurrection body would not have gender differences. In Mark 12:25, Jesus said, "In heaven they neither marry or are given in marriage."

It may be objected that the apostles clearly envisage male leadership and even female silence in church. Certainly the society they knew was patriarchal and had always been. Was this by divine ordering, or was God willing to achieve his purposes through life as it was? The argument just outlined might suggest the latter. In any case God seems to have made exceptions. Deborah was raised up as the leader of his people in the time of the Judges. Jesus did not choose any women in the twelve disciples, but as his primary mission was to the spiritual renewal of Israel the choice of twelve men could mirror the twelve patriarchs on whom the nation had been formed. A woman, Mary Magdalene, was chosen as the first apostle of the Resurrection. And in his earthly ministry Jesus gave greater attention to women than current society would afford. It was through a woman, Lydia, that the first church group in Europe was formed by Paul. The church was established in her house. Lydia can be regarded as its leader. What, then, should we make of the apostles' attitude to women leading in the church? The earlier exposition of the way Scripture is interpreted in this book is crucial here. While the apostles' exposition of the decisive act of God in Christ in his Death and Resurrection partakes of the finality of divine revelation, in matters more peripheral they reflect the culture and understanding of their time. And this was particularly true of their anthropology, their understanding of the history and ordering of humanity. We do not today follow what the New Testament writers say about the institution of slavery, an integral part of their society. Maybe when Paul wrote of distinctions no longer relevant "in Christ" he could not realize the full implications of that truth. Only centuries later, when history had moved on, would the principle in his words find greater fulfilment.

If after death it is the soul that lives on in heaven, a further question arises. How will it be made perfect for life in a perfect realm where no evil or sin may exist? The souls of those in Christ have been redeemed. The consequences of their fallen state have been removed by the atoning death of Christ. But even the most saintly who have died in old age are still imperfect, sinful, falling short of complete sanctification. How will God make us fit for the perfection of heaven?

The concept of purgatory grew in the Catholic and Orthodox Churches as an attempt to answer the problem. There was no support in the Bible, though use was made of a brief passage in one of the books of the Apocrypha, the second book of Maccabees. The idea was that by a period of suffering, longer or shorter according to the spiritual state of the individual, all that was unfit for heaven would be purged. Purgatory was not itself in heaven. It was thought that those who died in a state of perfection could go straight to heaven, though who could have achieved that state is impossible to say. By the prayers of priests, paid-for Masses and other gifts to the church the bereaved hoped to shorten time in Purgatory for their loved ones. The abuse of this system was a contributory stimulus for the Reformation.

Every believer, however saintly their life might be considered by others, is still short of perfection at the end of life. The sinful bias remains throughout life. Approximation to the sanctity of Christ is far from complete. How will God deal with this? We cannot really know. Paul in 1 Corinthians 15:52 speaks of us being changed "in the twinkling of an eye" at the Appearance of Christ. But the context there is really about the transformation of an earthly body into a spiritual resurrected body. In 1 John 3:2 the writer admits that we do not know what we shall be like in heaven, but when we see Christ we shall be like him, "for we shall see him as he is." This could be referring both to the body and the spirit. In regard to the latter, 2 Corinthians 3:18 speaks of being transformed into the likeness of Christ. There the emphasis is on character, spiritual development; but the process is to be going on in this life. Charles Wesley's hymn "Love Divine, All Loves Excelling" captures the idea: "Changed from glory into glory, 'till in Heaven we take our place." In these New Testament references the transformation comes about by beholding Christ. There are echoes here of Old Testament experiences. Moses spending time on Mount Sinai beholding the glory of Jehovah is seen afterwards transformed in appearance, bearing a supernatural glow. Although an experience of a different nature, Jesus on the Mount of Transfiguration is changed in appearance, shining with a supernatural light. Years afterwards Peter describing this event in 2 Peter 1:16–18 says, "We saw his greatness." Being close to Christ as he reveals the glory of God is thus a transforming experience. How and when that is complete for the believer, from the point of death to the final resurrection, we must leave to God. Of one thing we can be sure, he purposes to bring all his church, corporately and personally, to perfect sanctity in heaven.

So, when we are finally in heaven, what will it be like? We are sure of the negative truths. No more death, pain, partings, injustice, evil of any kind—discontinuity with our present life. There will be joy, perfect relationships, glory, glad worship of God. And, it is surely not presumptuous to suggest, there will be unending discovery of the mystery of God's majesty and greatness. On earth if we seek to know more of God's ways and will, we grow in holiness. May we see that as going on in heaven? In this life as we think about God we are always inclined to import into our concepts our own preferences. We picture God as we would like him to be. And some of our problems arise when God does not seem to confirm those desires. Exploring God in heaven will surely be free from unworthy motivations.

Will we know each other in heaven? The answer is surely yes, if relationships are then perfect. But, of course, it will not just be a gathering of old friends or relations. The whole church of God will be there. Looking at it from our present point of view, we may be enriched by knowing some of the great saints of history.

Some people taking too literally the pictures of heaven in the Bible and in art down the centuries have concluded it would be boring to be playing a harp endlessly. Or even, to be involved in endless worship. But that is to entertain an impoverished idea of worship. Through perfect worship of God we are ourselves fulfilled, finding our ultimate well-being, as well as giving due glory and praise to God. Some atheists ridicule the idea of a God demanding our worship. That shows how much they fail to understand God. They have created an image of God and then attacked it.

Whatever questions about heaven remain, and they will as long as we live, we may be confident that God will bring to completion his purposes from all eternity. He has not created this universe, not intervened in history, dealt with humanity with infinite patience, become incarnate in his Son, and at total cost to his love redeemed humanity, for it all to end in frustration and chaos. Throughout the whole of God's story, the rock on which it has been founded and built is his complete faithfulness. On that we place our hope. The Christian hope is not wishful thinking nor even a longed-for possibility, but a certainty as certain as God.

10

Epilogue

THIS BOOK has not been about proof that there is a God, supreme overall, if by proof is meant incontrovertible scientific proof. Nor has it offered proof that there is heaven. Each person has a choice to make, a choice of faith, of belief that there is God or there is not. As indicated at the beginning, we can choose to believe if our universe—the laws that have governed its expansion and evolution from the first moments, to the eventual appearance billions of years afterwards of *Homo sapiens* on a planet of a relatively small star—is simply a matter of chance, and there is no purpose in it all. Allied with that conclusion is the belief that a Mozart symphony, a Shakespeare play, a beautiful work of art, the capacity of humans to create amazingly complicated computers, to invent wonders of modern technology, and indeed to experience loving relationships, is solely a product of genes, chemical reactions, and electrical events in the brain. In this view there is no possibility that all these benefits reflect a creative ability derived from the creative action of a God in whose image humanity is made.

The other choice is to believe there is a supreme mind behind and sustaining all that is, that this God has a loving concern to relate to creatures capable of response, to believe that underlying all that has happened, is happening, and will happen is a purpose, often not perceived in detail but evident in certain key events in history. This understanding is outlined in the Bible, whose story has inner consistency and has convinced millions of people of all races, cultures, differences of personality down the centuries. Choosing to believe and respond to God in their own lives, they have been changed and found fulfilment.

11

The Last Journey—For You?

YOU ARE on a dark road. It is a one-way route. There is no turning back. The loving support of family and friends is fading from consciousness. But there is certainly clear awareness of a loving presence, supporting and guiding, so no fear. You come to a bend in the road. Turning it you come into glorious light and peace deeper than known before. And you are embraced by your Savior-God. He has brought you to the end he has planned from all eternity, and which he has procured at total cost to himself in self-sacrifice. Heaven.

If a further study of the issues in this book is desired there are books of outstanding merit and scholarship to which this writer is indebted. *The God of Hope and the End of the World* by John Polkinghorne (SPCK Publishing 2002) is by a world-class physicist who is also an Anglican priest. That book is a condensed summary of a symposium by scientists and theologians after a three-year study, published as *The End of the World and the End of God* (Trinity Press International 2000). Other books by John Polkinghorne are also most helpful.

On the crucial act of God in Christ, Jurgen Moltmann's *The Crucified God* (SCM Press 1974) and *Theology of Hope* (SCM Press 1967) and *The Resurrection of the Son of God* by N. T. Wright (SPCK Publishing 2003) have gained world-wide acclaim. Already referred to in this book is *Surprised by Hope* by N. T. Wright (SPCK Publishing 2007).

For anyone thinking about death, a wonderful book is *Enduring Melody* (Darton, Longman & Todd 2006) by Michael Mayne. It concerns his last months facing a terrible terminal cancer. Heaven is an offer no one can afford to refuse.